THE RETIREMENT CROSSWORD PUZZLE BOOK

OVER 100 QUICK CROSSWORD PUZZLES TO KEEP YOUR MIND ACTIVE

summersdale

THE RETIREMENT CROSSWORD PUZZLE BOOK

Text by Adam Ifans

An Hachette UK Company
www.hachette.co.uk

Summersdale Publishers
Part of Octopus Publishing Group Limited
Carmelite House
50 Victoria Embankment
LONDON
EC4Y 0DZ
UK

www.summersdale.com

Printed and bound in Malaysia

ISBN: 978-1-83799-341-3

Substantial discounts on bulk quantities of Summersdale books are available to corporations, professional associations and other organizations. For details contact general enquiries: telephone: +44 (0) 1243 771107 or email: enquiries@summersdale.com.

INTRODUCTION

Crossword puzzles are not merely time-fillers. They are powerful tools to sharpen your critical-thinking skills, increase your knowledge base and boost your memory. The benefits of this type of mental exercise become even more invaluable as we navigate the golden years of our lives.

The 116 puzzles in *The Retirement Crossword Puzzle Book* have been meticulously crafted to reflect the superior experience of those of us who are already retired, or on the verge of retirement. The topics span nine categories – movies and TV, popular culture, geography, food and drink, history and politics, sport, art and literature, music, and science and nature – mainly from the past seven decades, all in large print to enhance your puzzle-solving experience.

Consider this book your trustworthy companion in a vibrant phase of life, always here to offer you an entertaining challenge and a welcome trip down memory lane. Dive in, solve away and keep that intellectual spark ablaze!

CLASSIC AMERICAN TV SITCOMS

Can you remember all these prime-time laughathons?

ACROSS

3 Show about a large, blended musical family (3, 5, 5)

5 Dark comedy set during the Korean War (4)

6 This "show about nothing" is named after its comedian star (8)

DOWN

1 *Everyone Loves Lucy*, but what was her real name? (7, 4)

2 Name of the Boston bar where everybody knows your name (6)

4 Henry Winkler's character's nickname in *Happy Days* (6)

POPULAR CULTURE

GROOVY GADGETS FROM THE SIXTIES

Did these inventions stand the test of time?

ACROSS

4 Initials of machine invented in 1967 for convenient cash withdrawals (3)

6 A portable mathematical assistant (6, 10)

DOWN

1 Iconic fashion item – supplies are short! (4, 5)

2 Life-saving device for regulating a heartbeat (9)

3 There are _ _ _ _ _ tracks on this popular music storage medium (5)

5 Strong synthetic material used in bulletproof vests (6)

A CAPITAL ADVENTURE

Ah, the halcyon days of the atlas and the globe.
Let's see how well you remember the capitals
of the world. No Google Maps allowed!

ACROSS

3 Capital of Australia (8)

5 New Delhi is this
country's capital (5)

6 Capital of the United
States (10, 2)

DOWN

1 Capital of Argentina (6, 5)

2 Old capital of West
Germany (4)

4 Capital of the land of
the pyramids (5)

EATING YOUR WAY AROUND THE WORLD

Your suitcase may be well travelled, but are your taste buds?

ACROSS

1 Beetroot soup from Eastern Europe (7)

4 Japanese dish consisting of small rolls of vinegar-flavoured rice served with a garnish of raw fish, vegetables or egg (5)

5 Sweet pastry made of layers of filo filled with chopped nuts, popular in the Middle East and Greece (7)

6 German sausage made from pork, beef or veal (9)

DOWN

2 French buttery, flaky pastry of Austrian origin, named for its crescent shape (9)

3 Spanish dish made with rice, seafood and saffron (6)

BRR, IT'S A COLD WAR OUT THERE!

You've still got the key to your nuclear bunker, right?

ACROSS

1 Cuban _ _ _ _ _ _ _ _ _ _ _ _ _, 13-day confrontation between the US and the Soviet Union over munitions installations (7, 6)

4 Anti-communist hysteria in the US during the early years of the Cold War (11)

5 City and country divider that fell on 9 November 1989 (6, 4)

6 Soviet policy of open discussion of political and social issues, initiated by Mikhail Gorbachev in the 1980s (8)

DOWN

2 Metaphorical divider between the East and West during the Cold War (4, 7)

3 Competition for supremacy in nuclear warfare between the US and the Soviet Union (4, 4)

SPORT

GOING FOR GOLD

Buckle up for a sprint through some of the most iconic moments in Olympic sport. On your marks, get set, go!

ACROSS

3 Boxer who won light-heavyweight gold at the 1960 Olympics before becoming Muhammad Ali (7, 4)

4 Bob Beamon set a world record in this event in Mexico City in 1968 that stood for almost 23 years (4, 4)

6 Most decorated Olympian of all time, Michael _ _ _ _ _ _ (6)

DOWN

1 Revolutionary high-jump technique introduced in 1968 (7, 4)

2 Runner who had a famous fall in the 3,000 m race at the Los Angeles Olympics in 1984 (4, 6)

5 Romanian gymnast, _ _ _ _ _ Comăneci, who, in 1976, scored the first perfect ten (5)

ART AND LITERATURE

ONCE UPON A TIME

Time to revisit those magical worlds that shaped our childhoods and are still enchanting kids today.

ACROSS

3 Residence of Mr Toad in *The Wind in the Willows* (4, 4)

5 The lion in *The Chronicles of Narnia* (5)

6 Where Alice ended up after following the White Rabbit (10)

DOWN

1 Colourful home of Anne Shirley (5, 6)

2 The man-cub raised by wolves in *The Jungle Book* (6)

4 They live with Peter in Neverland (4, 4)

DANCE FAVOURITES FROM THE SEVENTIES

Dig out your flares, it's time to disco!

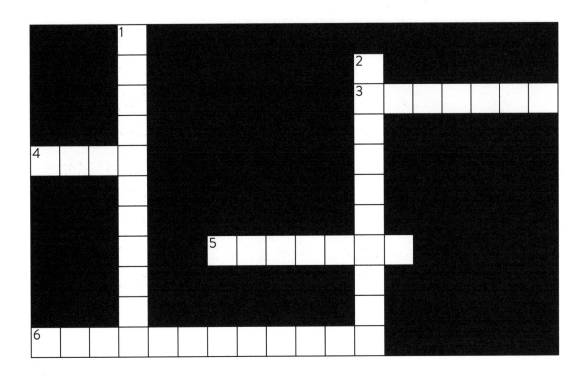

ACROSS

3 Hit song by The Trammps, "Disco _ _ _ _ _ _ _" (7)

4 Village People anthem accompanied by arm choreography (4)

5 Smiley trio behind "Stayin' Alive" (3, 4)

6 Singer of the iconic song "I Will Survive" (6, 6)

DOWN

1 Singer known as the "Queen of Disco" (5, 6)

2 John Travolta played the dancing lead in the hit movie *Saturday* _ _ _ _ _ _ _ _ _ _ (5, 5)

BLAST OFF!

Put down your reading glasses and put on your flight helmet – it's time to join the space race.

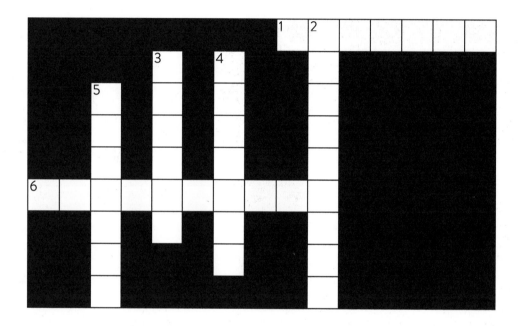

ACROSS

1 First human to journey into outer space (7)

6 Space shuttle tragically lost in 1986 (10)

DOWN

2 First person to walk on the moon (9)

3 Space telescope launched in 1990 (6)

4 First artificial Earth satellite, launched by the USSR (7)

5 Unmanned spacecraft that took the first detailed pictures of Jupiter and Saturn (7)

BLONDE AMBITION

Time for a little glitz and glamour, as we shine the spotlight on a true icon – Marilyn Monroe.

ACROSS

2 Magazine that featured her as its first cover girl (7)

4 Sport played by her second husband, Joe DiMaggio (8)

5 Movie where she plays Sugar Kane and sings "I Wanna Be Loved By You" (4, 4, 2, 3)

6 President to whom Marilyn sang "Happy Birthday" (7)

DOWN

1 Marilyn Monroe's birth forenames (5, 5)

3 Artist who created a famously colourful portrait series of Marilyn (6)

CURTAIN UP

The smell of the greasepaint, the roar of the crowd, let's see how well you recall these showstopping musicals.

ACROSS

4 Andrew Lloyd Webber musical based on T. S. Eliot poems (4)

5 Rodgers and Hammerstein's first collaboration (8)

6 Demon barber of Fleet Street (7, 4)

DOWN

1 Musical adaptation of *Pygmalion* (2, 4, 4)

2 *Mamma Mia!* features the songs of this pop group (4)

3 Musical that tells the backstory of the witches in *The Wizard of Oz* (6)

GEOGRAPHY

WORLD FAMOUS LANDMARKS

Grab your passport, it's time to revisit some favourite haunts from around the globe.

ACROSS

5 Ancient Roman amphitheatre (9)

6 Gift from France to the United States (6, 2, 7)

DOWN

1 Longest man-made structure, found in China (5, 4)

2 Mausoleum in Agra, India (3, 5)

3 Prehistoric monument in England (10)

4 Tower that's a symbol of Paris (6)

FOOD AND DRINK

SHAKEN, NOT STIRRED

Remember when a cocktail party was the social event of the week? Here's a crossword that's sure to lift your spirits.

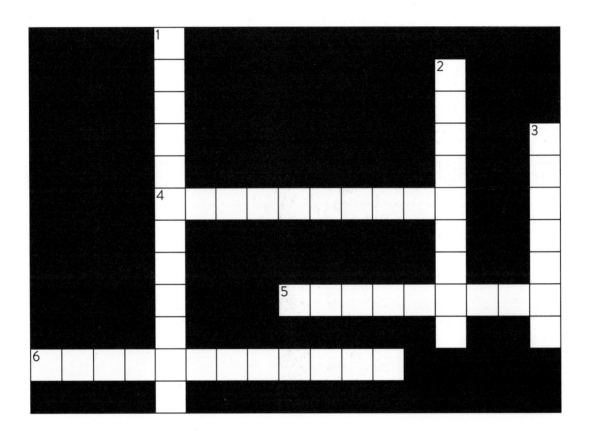

ACROSS

4 Tropical cocktail with rum, coconut and pineapple (4, 6)

5 Whisky cocktail named after a New York borough (9)

6 Whisky cocktail that's less outdated than its name might suggest (3, 9)

DOWN

1 Vodka cocktail made famous by *Sex and the City* (12)

2 Tequila-based drink often served with salt (9)

3 Classic cocktail often garnished with an olive (7)

ICONIC LEADERS

Love 'em or hate 'em, there's no way you
can forget these figures from history.

ACROSS

3 Leader of India's non-violent
independence movement (6)

5 Mao Zedong's original title
as leader of the Chinese
Communist Party (8)

6 US president known for
the New Deal (9)

DOWN

1 Leader of the Bolshevik
Revolution (5)

2 South African president who
fought against apartheid (7)

4 French president who led the
Free French forces (2, 6)

 **SPORT**

MATCH POINT

Get ready for a grand slam of tennis trivia in this smashing puzzle.

ACROSS

4 Famous for the phrase "You cannot be serious!" (7)

5 Oldest tennis tournament in the world (9)

6 Surface of the French Open courts (4)

DOWN

1 Type of stroke hit with the rear of the hand facing the ball (8)

2 Swiss player with 20 Grand Slam titles (7)

3 Younger of the championship-winning Williams sisters (6)

BON VOYAGE

Travel literature is your armchair ticket to far-off lands but how well do you know your classics? Buckle up!

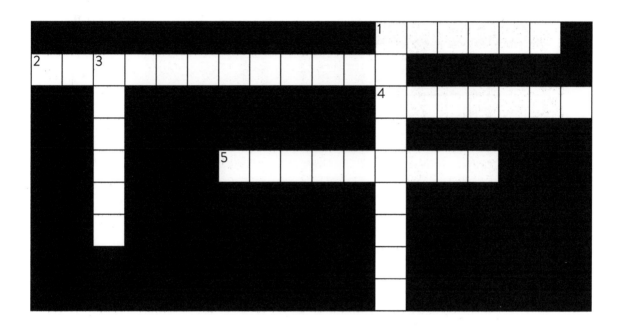

ACROSS

1 Wrote *Down and Out in Paris and London* (6)

2 Bill Bryson wrote about this country in *Notes on a Small Island* (5, 7)

4 Author of *The Pillars of Hercules* (7)

5 Mark Twain wrote *The _ _ _ _ _ _ _ _ _ Abroad* (9)

DOWN

1 Jack Kerouac's first novel, about a journey (2, 3, 4)

3 Number of days it took to go around the world in Jules Verne's novel (6)

MUSIC, MAESTRO!

Whether you're a virtuoso or simply a fan of the classics, these clues are sure to be music to your ears. Encore!

ACROSS

4 You might find this ballet by Tchaikovsky useful in the kitchen (3, 10)

5 German composer of *The Ring Cycle* (6)

6 Famous opera by Bizet (6)

DOWN

1 Wrote the opera *The Magic Flute* (6)

2 Composer of the *Moonlight Sonata* (9)

3 Vivaldi wrote *The Four _ _ _ _ _ _ _* (7)

COMPUTERS BYTE BACK

Remember when you had to plug your home computer into the television? Let's download some more digital memories.

ACROSS

3 Not a hard disk? (6)

5 Early search engine featuring a butler (3, 6)

6 Early gaming-console company (5)

DOWN

1 Creator of MS-DOS and Windows operating systems (9)

2 Social-networking precursor to Facebook (7)

4 Sinclair's first colour computer (8)

FLASHBACK TO CULT CLASSICS

Hit rewind on your VCR and see how many
of these classic movies you know.

ACROSS

4 Movie with Al Pacino's iconic
role as Tony Montana, a
Cuban gangster in Miami (8)

6 A midnight *Picture Show*
with time warps (5, 6)

DOWN

1 Terry Gilliam's
dystopian satire (6)

2 The Dude abides in *The
Big _ _ _ _ _ _ _ _* (8)

3 Dark comedy about
high-school cliques (8)

5 The brothers responsible for
crime comedy *Fargo* (4)

ICONS OF FASHION

Put on your best outfit and get ready to strut your stuff on the crossword catwalk!

ACROSS

2 Iconic sixties model with a pixie cut (6)

6 French designer known for the "little black dress" (4, 6)

DOWN

1 British supermodel who was sometimes in the soup (8)

3 Italian luxury brand with a double G logo (5)

4 Supposedly, *The Devil Wears _ _ _ _ _* (5)

5 Fashion magazine where Wintour reigns (5)

 **GEOGRAPHY**

SCALING THE HEIGHTS

This puzzle will have you feeling on top of the world – just don't look down!

ACROSS

4 Home to the world's highest mountain (9)

5 The Pyrenees divide France and _ _ _ _ _ (5)

6 European skiing paradise (4)

DOWN

1 South American range (5)

2 The Atlas Mountains stretch across three countries in this continent (6)

3 Country at the northernmost tip of the Rockies (6)

FOOD AND DRINK

SUNNY SIDE UP

They say it's the most important meal of the day, so here's a toast to American breakfasts.

ACROSS

3 Southern corn dish (5)

5 A doughnut's bready cousin (5)

6 Eggy bread that isn't as Parisian as it sounds (6, 5)

DOWN

1 Shredded potato dish (4, 6)

2 Flat morning delight, served with maple syrup (8)

4 Fluffy in the US, crunchy in the UK (8)

THE CUBAN REVOLUTION

Put down your cigars and mojitos – it's time to see if your knowledge is as strong as a cup of Cuban coffee.

ACROSS

2 Capital city where much of the revolution was centred (6)

4 He led the Cuban Revolution (5, 6)

6 The Cuban dictator overthrown in 1959 (7)

DOWN

1 Failed post-revolution invasion attempt backed by the US (3, 2, 4)

3 Type of warfare used by the revolutionaries (9)

5 _ _ _ Guevara, Argentinian revolutionary who played a key role in the Cuban Revolution (3)

FLOAT LIKE A BUTTERFLY, SOLVE LIKE A BEE

Let's see if you can bob and weave through these clues like a true champ.

ACROSS

1 A left-handed boxer (8)

4 Strategy famously used by Ali against George Foreman (4-1-4)

5 Boxer known for a notorious ear-biting incident (5)

DOWN

1 Sweet names of Leonard and Robinson, both boxing legends (5, 3)

2 "The Greatest" in boxing history (3)

3 Do this to finish the fight early (5, 3)

A PICTURE PAINTS A THOUSAND WORDS

Do you need to brush up your art knowledge or do you have a palette of answers ready to go?

ACROSS

4 Surreal Salvador's surname (4)

5 Van Gogh's celestial masterpiece (6, 5)

6 Mexican painter Kahlo's first name (5)

DOWN

1 Da Vinci's enigmatic lady (4, 4)

2 Warhol was a pioneer in this movement (3, 3)

3 Picasso's groundbreaking movement (6)

POP GOES THE EIGHTIES

Strap on your leg warmers and tease up that hair – it's time to test your knowledge of the golden age of pop.

ACROSS

4 Prince's colourful downpour (6, 4)

6 Kenny Loggins' dance anthem (9)

DOWN

1 Duo that gave us "Wake Me Up Before You Go-Go" (4)

2 Singer of "Girls Just Want To Have Fun" (5, 6)

3 Singer who'll never give you up (4, 6)

5 Band who were "Livin' on a Prayer" (3, 4)

FANGS FOR THE MEMORIES

It's eat or be eaten in the animal kingdom, so see if you can sink your teeth into these clues about predatory animals.

ACROSS

3 Largest lizard that hunts in Indonesia, the Komodo _ _ _ _ _ _ (6)

4 Canine known for its pack-hunting behaviour (4)

5 The US's feathered national symbol (4, 5)

6 Venomous spider with a deadly reputation (5, 5)

DOWN

1 The Nile's most notorious predator (9)

2 Shark species featured in *Jaws* (5, 5)

EALING COMEDIES

These classic films put British humour on the world map. Let's see if you can crack these clues without cracking up!

ACROSS

3 A mob of retirees pull off a heist in *The _ _ _ _ _ _ _ _ _ _ _ _ Mob* (8, 4)

5 The garment worn in a film about an indestructible fabric (5, 4)

6 Criminals meet their match in an old lady (3, 11)

DOWN

1 Country that was the setting for a wartime film about an island with a whisky shortage (8)

2 Star of *Kind Hearts and Coronets* – and *Star Wars* (4, 8)

4 A London district declares independence, *Passport to _ _ _ _ _ _ _* (7)

TOYS AND GAMES

Classic toys and games that you'd still play with, given half a chance. Ready to roll the dice on this one?

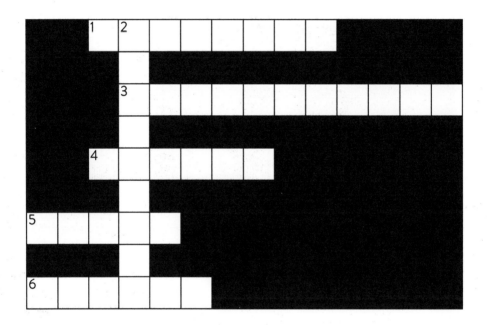

ACROSS

1 Board game with a jail and four railway stations (8)

3 Draw without ink or paper (4, 1, 6)

4 The iconic doll (6)

5 Ernő _ _ _ _ _, inventor of the colourful cube of a puzzle (5)

6 A toy that "walks" down stairs (6)

DOWN

2 Game where you get to be a surgeon for the day (9)

 GEOGRAPHY

INSPIRING ISLANDS

Whether you've visited them or just dreamed about it, it's time to set sail on a crossword adventure!

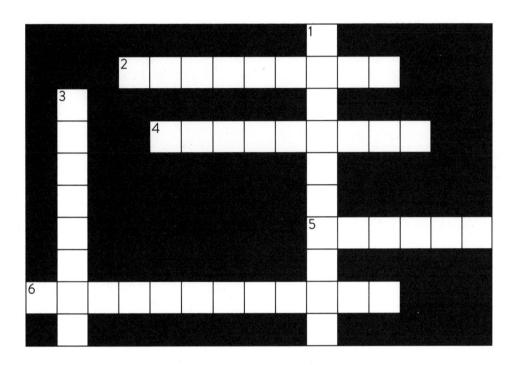

ACROSS

2 World's largest island, not counting Australia (9)

4 Islands where Darwin spent a lot of time (9)

5 Largest island in the Mediterranean (6)

6 Canada's most easterly island (12)

DOWN

1 Island nation off the coast of Africa, west of Mauritius (10)

3 Nation in the Indian Ocean formed of 1,192 islands (8)

FOOD AND DRINK

WOK AND ROLL

Time to get stuck into some delicious Chinese cuisine. Let's see if you can stir-fry your way through these tasty clues!

ACROSS

2 Chinese dumplings, often in soup (6)

5 Classic blend of seasonings (4-5)

6 A Beijing speciality, it's a quacker (6, 4)

DOWN

1 Sweet end to a meal with a mysterious message (7, 6)

3 Stir-fried noodles (4, 4)

4 Small Cantonese dishes, often served with tea (3, 3)

HISTORY AND POLITICS

NOBEL PURSUITS

Can you figure out these Nobel Prize-winning creative and intellectual giants?

ACROSS

3 First woman to win a Nobel Prize (5, 5)

5 Civil-rights leader with a dream (4)

6 First songwriter to win a Nobel Prize for Literature (3, 5)

DOWN

1 Scientist known for his obedient dogs (6)

2 Author of *The Old Man and the Sea* (9)

4 South African Peace Prize winner who started the nineties in prison (7)

FORMULA ONE

Buckle your seatbelt and let's see if you've got the drive to succeed in this puzzle.

ACROSS

3 Iconic Italian racing team (7)

4 A zigzag on the track (7)

5 Starting point for the fastest qualifier (4, 8)

6 Where cars get quick service (3, 4)

DOWN

1 Main Formula One racing event (5, 4)

2 Famous street circuit (6)

CLASSIC COMIC STRIPS

A newspaper wouldn't be a newspaper without
a comic strip to make readers chuckle.

ACROSS

3 A boy and his stuffed tiger (6, 3, 6)

5 A cat who quite simply loves lasagne (8)

6 A Great Dane full of even greater antics (9)

DOWN

1 Surreal single-panel humour by Gary Larson (3, 3, 4)

2 Charlie Brown's canine companion (6)

4 Featuring Peppermint Patty, Woodstock and Pig-Pen (7)

MUCK, MUD AND MUSIC

Break out the glitter, it's time to put up your tent and chill out to some famous music festivals.

ACROSS

2 Informal name for boots worn at rainy UK music festivals (7)

5 Country where the Montreux Jazz Festival is held (11)

6 Possibly the most feared place at any music festival: the portable _ _ _ _ _ _ (6)

DOWN

1 The UK's largest music festival (11)

3 Iconic 1969 festival in the US (9)

4 Type of music played at the Monsters of Rock festival (5, 5)

SCIENCE AND NATURE

SURF'S UP

Who says you can't teach an old dog new clicks?
Let's navigate the World Wide Web, one clue at a time!

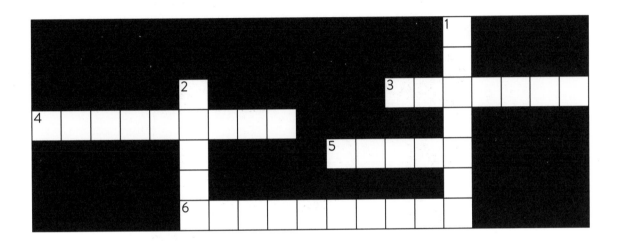

ACROSS

3 Tasty data files stored by websites (7)

4 Watching video in real time (9)

5 Something, usually nasty, that is spread rapidly online (5)

6 Social-media celebrity (10)

DOWN

1 Chrome or Firefox, for example (7)

2 Digital expression of emotion (5)

FUR, FEATHERS AND FANGS

Who needs human actors when you've got the animal stars to feature in your films? Let's dive into the wildlife of Hollywood!

ACROSS

1 Pig who wants to be a sheepdog (4)

2 Harry Potter's snowy owl (6)

4 Dorothy's dog in *The Wizard of Oz* (4)

5 Intelligent bottlenose dolphin (7)

DOWN

1 St Bernard who causes comedy chaos (9)

3 Famous collie who always saves the day (6)

POPULAR CULTURE

START YOUR ENGINES

Who says you need a driver's licence to take a trip down memory lane? Buckle up for a puzzle ride through classic cars!

ACROSS

2 Ford's wild horse (7)

3 Iconic British compact car, famous for *The Italian Job* (4)

4 Luxury carmaker, manufacturer of the Silver Ghost (5-5)

5 Volkswagen's bug-shaped vehicle (6)

DOWN

1 Synonymous with American automotive luxury (8)

3 Ford's game-changing vehicle (5, 1)

NATIONAL PARKS

No need for hiking boots or a compass when you can explore the USA's most stunning scenery from the comfort of your crossword grid.

ACROSS

2 Home to the Old Faithful geyser (11)

4 California's Sequoia National Park is home to the giant _ _ _ _ _ _ _ _ _ _ _ (7, 4)

5 This US canyon isn't just big, it's _ _ _ _ _ (5)

6 Famous for the El Capitan rock formation (8)

DOWN

1 The hottest and driest national park in the US (5, 6)

3 Florida's swampy reserve (10)

FOOD AND DRINK

BON APPÉTIT

Grab your knife and fork – and maybe a pen! – for this culinary tour of classic French cuisine.

ACROSS

3 Shell-shaped sponge cake that famously evoked Proust's memories (9)

5 Chicken cooked in red wine (3, 2, 3)

6 Upside-down apple tart (5, 5)

DOWN

1 Home city of bouillabaisse, the classic fish stew (9)

2 Duck and bean casserole (9)

4 Nutty ingredient in a *macaron* (6)

WORLD WAR TWO

Prepare to deploy your wits as we navigate the history of the world's biggest conflict.

ACROSS

3 Second atomic bomb target (8)

4 German encryption machine (6)

5 Supreme Allied Commander (10)

6 Site of evacuation of British troops (7)

DOWN

1 Site of a pivotal Soviet victory (10)

2 French government under Nazi control (5)

SPORT

BACK OF THE NET

Ready to tackle some clues? Let's kick off a journey back to the football heroes of the seventies.

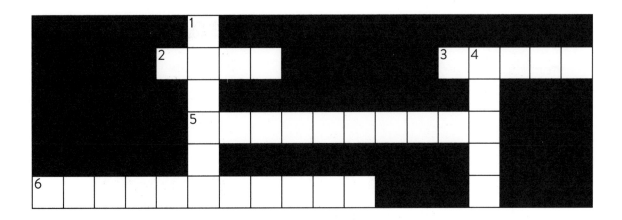

ACROSS

2 Brazilian superstar who retired in 1977 (4)

3 Goalkeeper Dino Zoff was a World Cup winner with this country (5)

5 Northern Irish winger for Manchester United (6, 4)

6 German defender, also known as "Der Kaiser" (11)

DOWN

1 Kevin _ _ _ _ _ _, English forward who played for Liverpool (6)

4 Johan Cruyff was a master of "_ _ _ _ _ Football" (5)

WHODUNNIT?

Get your little grey cells working with some mysteries from the golden age of detective fiction.

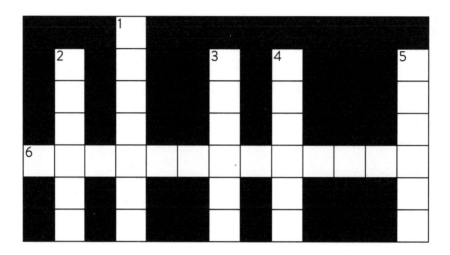

ACROSS

6 Train on which a famous murder occurred (6, 7)

DOWN

1 Surname of the author of *The Maltese Falcon* (7)

2 Belgian detective with a famous moustache (6)

3 Dorothy L. _ _ _ _ _ _, creator of Lord Peter Wimsey (6)

4 Knitting sleuth from St Mary Mead (6)

5 Holmes's loyal friend (6)

LET'S ROCK!

Crank up the volume to 11 and get ready to crack these clues.

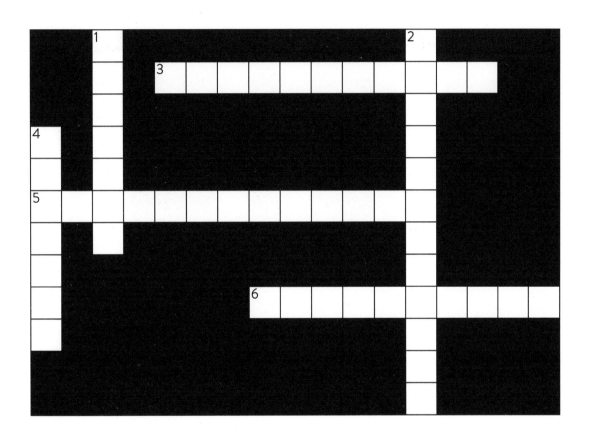

ACROSS

3 Band that gave us "Whole Lotta Love" (3, 8)

5 Band that gathered no moss (7, 6)

6 Ziggy Stardust's alter ego (5, 5)

DOWN

1 Pink Floyd's stack of bricks (3, 4)

2 Ozzy Osbourne's original band (5, 7)

4 Queen Freddy's surname (7)

A DOSE OF MEDICAL MARVELS

Are you ready to operate on these clues? Scalpel, please!

ACROSS

1 Antibiotic discovered by Fleming (10)

4 Inert medicine used in trials (7)

5 Dolly the sheep was the first (5)

DOWN

1 Heartbeat regulator (9)

2 Hormone for diabetes treatment (7)

3 Medical procedure where an egg is fertilized outside the body (3)

FRIGHTS AND DELIGHTS

Don't be scared, it's just a crossword. But maybe keep the lights on, just in case, while you wrestle with these classic horror movies.

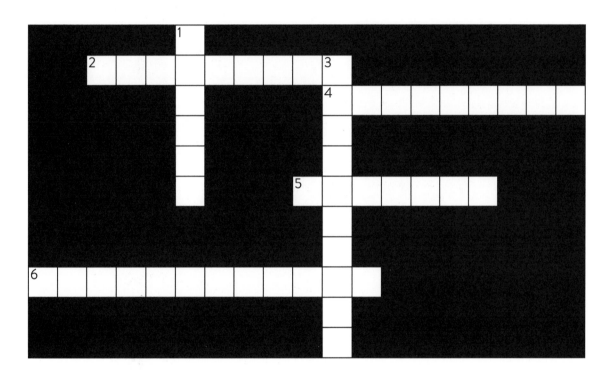

ACROSS

2 Freddy's nightmare domain (3, 5)

4 Michael Myers' favourite time of the year (9)

5 Bad luck follows this child (3, 4)

6 The name of the scientist, not the monster (12)

DOWN

1 Hitchcock's motel thriller (6)

3 "Here's Johnny!" (3, 7)

MAD MEN

Can you match up these advertising slogans from the seventies, eighties and nineties with the brands they're promoting?

ACROSS

3 "The choice of a new generation" (5)

4 Initials for "finger-lickin' good" (3)

5 In the US, it was "Plop, plop, fizz, fizz" (4-7)

6 "The best a man can get" (8)

DOWN

1 "Maybe she's born with it" (10)

2 "It's the real thing" (4-4)

DIVE INTO THE DEEP

Ready to navigate the world's oceans and seas without leaving your armchair? Let's set sail!

ACROSS

2 Moses parted this (3, 3)

5 A warm ocean current in the Atlantic (4, 6)

6 You can float easily here (4, 3)

DOWN

1 The only sea without a shore (8)

3 Bordered by six countries including Russia and Turkey (5, 3)

4 The largest ocean on Earth (7)

SUGAR RUSH

Classic confectionery and sweets that never go out of style.

ACROSS

4 A chocolate-covered bar from another planet (4)

5 A triangular taste sensation (9)

6 Old name for Snickers in the UK (8)

DOWN

1 A sweet mouthful that can seem everlasting (10)

2 Colourful beans and babies are made of this (5)

3 French company famous for gummy bears (6)

SCANDALOUS AFFAIRS

Ready to dig into some of the most infamous moments in political history? No cover-ups here, just clues!

ACROSS

3 Nixon's undoing (9)

5 UK newspaper that closed after a phone-hacking scandal (4, 2, 3, 5)

6 House of Commons financial scandal, "_ _ _ _ _ _ _ Questions" (4, 3)

DOWN

1 Reagan-era arms-deal scandal (4-6)

2 Clinton's infamous affair with Monica _ _ _ _ _ _ _ _ (8)

4 British minister who had an affair with a model in the sixties (7)

SPORT

SWING INTO ACTION

Get ready to putt your way through golf history, one clue at a time. No mulligans allowed!

ACROSS

3 Masters course in the US (7)

4 Australian golfer known as the "Great White Shark" (4, 6)

5 Biennial professional men's competition between Europe and the US (5, 3)

6 Spanish golfer with unrivalled flair (4, 11)

DOWN

1 Known as the "Golden Bear" (4, 8)

2 The "Home of Golf" in Scotland (2, 7)

FROM PAGE TO SCREEN

Dive into the world of literary bestsellers that made it big in Hollywood.

ACROSS

3 Helen Fielding's diary-writer (7, 5)

5 Civil War epic that won eight Oscars (4, 4, 3, 4)

6 The prison in Stephen King's redemptive tale (9)

DOWN

1 Michael Crichton's dinosaurs run amok (8, 4)

2 Mafia saga by Mario Puzo (3, 9)

4 Palahniuk's tale of underground brawls (5, 4)

ROCK AROUND THE CLOCK

Time to twist and shout through the golden era of rock 'n' roll, jazz and pop.

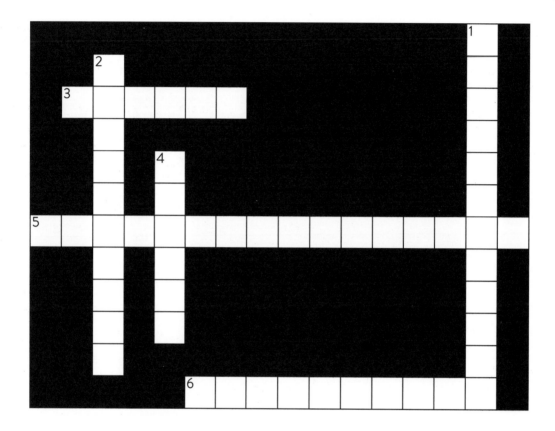

ACROSS

3 _ _ _ _ _ _ Holiday, jazz singer known for her "Strange Fruit" (6)

5 Jerry Lee Lewis's hottest hit (5, 5, 2, 4)

6 Early style of rock and roll (10)

DOWN

1 The King of Rock 'n' Roll (5, 7)

2 Ella _ _ _ _ _ _ _ _ _ _, the First Lady of Song (10)

4 Detroit-based record label (6)

A LEAFY ADVENTURE

Let's branch out and examine some of the world's trees, one crossword clue at a time.

ACROSS

4 Animal that finds the eucalyptus tree particularly tasty (5)

5 Tropical tree bearing coconuts (4)

6 Miniature tree art from Japan (6)

DOWN

1 Teary tree found near water

2 African "Tree of Life" (6)

3 Source of syrup and autumn colours (5)

CLASSIC ANIMATION

Do you have what it takes to solve these cartoon clues?

ACROSS

2 Disney's magical, musical masterpiece (8)

4 Bambi's rabbit friend (7)

5 The fairest of them all (4, 5)

6 Foxy hero of Sherwood Forest (5, 4)

DOWN

1 Breed coveted by Cruella de Vil (9)

3 Wielder of the magic lamp (7)

NOT SO SOCIAL MEDIA

Ready to slide into the DMs of this crossword?
Don't worry, no selfies required!

ACROSS

1 Symbol used to categorize posts (7)

4 Someone who subscribes to your social-media feed (8)

6 What's currently popular online (8)

DOWN

2 Behind-the-scenes sorter of your social-media feed (9)

3 Before it became X, to share someone else's Twitter post (7)

5 Digital thumbs-up (4)

DESERT STORM

The most barren places on Earth, deserts are where survival is a challenge. Let's embark on a journey through the most fascinating of them!

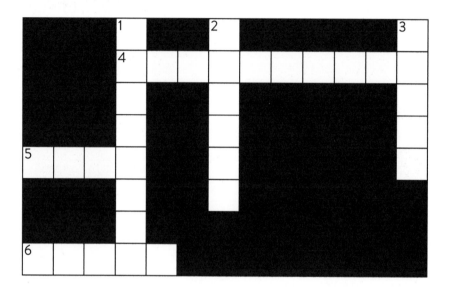

ACROSS

4 The world's coldest desert (10)

5 US state in the north-east corner of the Mojave Desert (4)

6 A fertile spot in a desert (5)

DOWN

1 African desert with the Okavango Delta (8)

2 Largest desert in Africa (6)

3 The ship of the desert (5)

FOOD AND DRINK

A CULINARY TOUR OF ITALY

Whether you're a gourmand or a casual diner, this crossword is your ticket to Italy – no passport required!

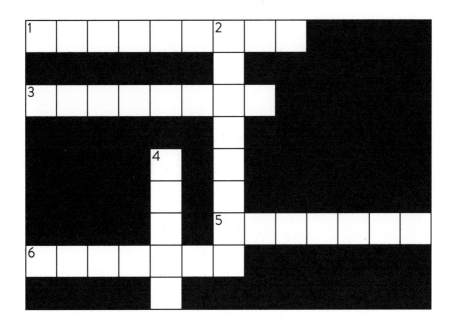

ACROSS

1 Christmas cake (9)

3 Strong coffee (8)

5 Folded pizza (7)

6 Creamy rice dish (7)

DOWN

2 Braised veal shanks (4, 4)

4 Basil-based sauce (5)

CHINA'S CULTURAL REVOLUTION

It was a period that changed the face of China and left an indelible mark on history. Let's see what you remember about this transformative era.

ACROSS

3 Areas of collectivized living and working (8)

4 Collection of the leader's quotations (6, 3, 4)

5 Removal of perceived enemies (5)

6 Youth paramilitary organization that enforced policies (3, 5)

DOWN

1 Extreme adoration of a leader, the Cult of _ _ _ _ _ _ _ _ _ _ _ (11)

2 Western name of the capital city at the start of the Cultural Revolution (6)

SPORT

BRING ON THE BASEBALL

Step up to the plate and see if you can hit a home run on these questions.

ACROSS

5 A _ _ _ _ _ _ of Their Own, movie about a women's baseball league during World War Two (6)

6 Annual championship showdown (5, 6)

DOWN

1 The Sultan of Swat, _ _ _ _ Ruth (4)

2 Book and film about Oakland Athletics starring Brad Pitt (9)

3 New York's American League team (7)

4 They throw the ball at the batter (7)

GREAT GALLERIES AND MUSEUMS

The world's great art galleries and museums are a feast for the eyes and soul. Let's brush up on our art history, shall we?

ACROSS

1 A collection of museums in Washington, DC (11)

4 Home to the *Mona Lisa* in Paris (6)

6 London home of the Rosetta Stone (7, 6)

DOWN

2 New York's art giant (12)

3 Famous for its spiral structure in New York (10)

5 London's "modern" art hub (4)

BRILLIANT BRITPOP

Cast your mind back to the nineties and a time of Union Jacks and guitar tracks. Let's rock!

ACROSS

3 Cool _ _ _ _ _ _ _ _ _: term capturing the UK's cultural boom in the nineties (9)

4 Pulp's charismatic frontman (6, 6)

5 Last name of the feuding brothers in Oasis (9)

6 Band behind "Bitter Sweet Symphony" (5)

DOWN

1 Iconic album by Blur (8)

2 UK's equivalent of the Grammys (4, 6)

AN AQUATIC ADVENTURE

Ready to explore the ocean's wonders? Let's dive in!

ACROSS

1 Crustacean that attaches to ships (8)

3 This equine fish's male carries the eggs (8)

4 Known for its long, spiral tusk (7)

5 Underwater ecosystem known as the rainforest of the sea (5, 4)

DOWN

1 Largest animal on Earth (4, 5)

2 Tiny creatures on which whales feast (5)

CLASSIC WAR MOVIES

Lights, camera, gunfire – it's time for
the silver screen's bravest battles.

ACROSS

3 Film featuring Steve McQueen's wartime motorcycle jump (3, 5, 6)

4 Oliver Stone's *Platoon* was set in this country (7)

5 A team of 12 misfit soldiers (3, 5, 5)

6 Setting for *Das Boot* (1-4)

DOWN

1 Vietnam War film inspired by *Heart of Darkness* (10, 3)

2 Saved by Spielberg's D-Day epic (7, 4)

GADGETS IN THE NOUGHTIES

The 2000s – the decade when flip phones were cool and Wi-Fi was a novelty. It's time for tech!

ACROSS

2 Nintendo's way to make gamers out of grandparents (3)

4 Maker of the Xbox 360 (9)

6 Successor to DVDs (3-3)

DOWN

1 The original fruity smartphone (10)

3 Apple's pocket jukebox (4)

5 Palm_ _ _ _ _, a personal organizer before smartphones (5)

JET-SETTER JUMBLE

Pack your bags and prepare for a crossword tour of the world's top getaway destinations.

ACROSS

5 Greek island with stunning sunsets (9)

6 City of light – and love (5)

DOWN

1 Volcanic US archipelago in the Pacific (6)

2 Indonesian island paradise (4)

3 French Polynesian paradise (6)

4 Japan's cultural heart (5)

SWEET-TOOTH DELIGHTS

Take a mouth-watering tour through the world of cakes, bakes and desserts.

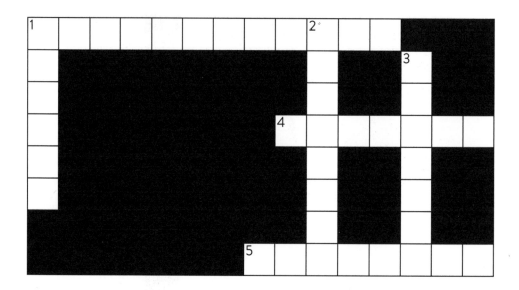

ACROSS

1 Pancake from France, flambéed with orange-flavoured spirit (5, 7)

4 Meringue dessert named after a Russian ballerina (7)

5 A beignet is a New-Orleans-style _ _ _ _ _ _ _ _ (8)

DOWN

1 Single Spanish fried-dough pastry (6)

2 Italian coffee-flavoured dessert (8)

3 German Christmas bread (7)

HISTORY AND POLITICS

THE GULF WAR

No need for night-vision goggles on this crossword battlefield.

ACROSS

2 US General: "Stormin'
_____" Schwarzkopf (6)

3 Resource at the centre of Middle East conflict (3)

5 Operation that liberated Kuwait (6, 5)

DOWN

1 Restricted airspace (2, 3, 4)

4 Iraqi leader at the time (6)

6 Iraqi ballistic missile (4)

SCRUM DOWN

Can you tackle these rugby-union riddles as thrilling as a last-minute try? No need for a mouthguard – just your thinking cap and a pen!

ACROSS

4 Gareth _ _ _ _ _ _ _, scorer of a legendary try in 1973 (7)

5 British and Irish combined touring team (5)

6 War dance performed by All Blacks (4)

DOWN

1 Last line of defence (4-4)

2 Ejection from the game (3, 4)

3 Points scored by attackers grounding the ball in goal (5)

ART AND LITERATURE

LITERARY TIME TRAVEL

Dive into the pages of history without leaving your armchair.

ACROSS

3 James Clavell's novel set in feudal Japan (6)

4 Mantel's lauded story about Thomas Cromwell (4, 4)

6 Medieval murder mystery by Umberto Eco (3, 4, 2, 3, 4)

DOWN

1 *The Three* _ _ _ _ _ _ _ _ _ _, a tale of swashbuckling soldiers (10)

2 The Napoleonic wars, according to Leo Tolstoy (3, 3, 5)

5 Household position of the central character in *The Remains of the Day* (6)

MUSIC

CLASSIC ALBUMS

If you're a music aficionado, this crossword will have you humming along in no time.

ACROSS

2 *The Dark Side of ___ ____*, the title of Pink Floyd's psychedelic masterpiece (3, 4)

4 There are *Rumours* this band topped the charts in 1977 (9, 3)

5 Art Garfunkel's partner on "Bridge Over Troubled Water" (4, 5)

6 Bruce Springsteen's breakthrough hit single on his album of the same name (4, 2, 3)

DOWN

1 Marvin Gaye's soulful enquiry (5, 5, 2)

3 The Beatles' 1969 classic (5, 4)

ASTRONOMICAL SIGHTS

Time to take a cosmic journey through the mysteries of the universe.

ACROSS

3 The galaxy we call home (5, 3)

5 An eruption from the sun (5, 5)

6 Mars, also known as the _ _ _ Planet (3)

DOWN

1 A dark point of no return (5, 4)

2 Largest planet in our solar system (7)

4 A belt between Mars and Jupiter (8)

LEGENDS OF COMEDY

Nothing beats a good laugh, but can you work out these comic geniuses?

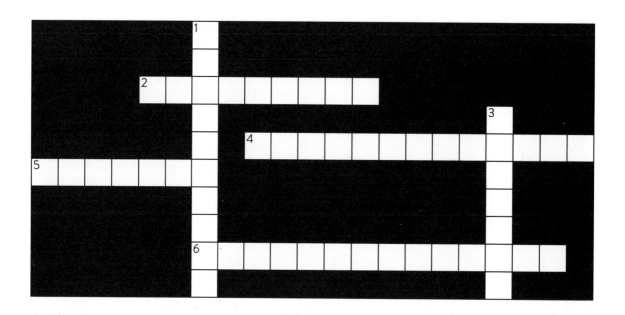

ACROSS

2 *Blazing Saddles* director (3, 6)

4 Mork, not Mindy (5, 8)

5 Starred in seven *Road to ...* movies with Bing Crosby (3, 4)

6 *Sister Act* star (6, 8)

DOWN

1 She went *Overboard* with Kurt Russell (6, 4)

3 *30 Rock* creator (4, 3)

POPULAR CULTURE

STARS FROM THE SIXTIES

Get ready to groove with the celebrities who truly made the sixties swing.

ACROSS

3 Barbara Streisand won an Oscar for this movie (5, 4)

5 Pop-art pioneer (4, 6)

6 *Cleopatra* star (9, 6)

DOWN

1 Rudolf Nureyev's profession (6, 6)

2 Played "The Star-Spangled Banner" at Woodstock (4, 7)

4 "Blowin' in the Wind" singer-songwriter (3, 5)

AMAZING ASIA

It's the largest continent in the world but how much do you know about its geography?

ACROSS

4 Capital of China (7)

5 Body of water between India and the Arabian peninsula (7, 3)

6 Japanese warrior class (7)

DOWN

1 Land of Genghis Khan (8)

2 Ancient trade route (4, 4)

3 Russian region known for its cold (7)

SPANISH CUISINE

Ready to tickle your taste buds? Let's tuck into the delicious world of Spanish cuisine.

ACROSS

3 Cold tomato soup (8)

5 Bean stew from Asturias (6)

6 Spanish spiced pork, similar to Italy's salami (7)

DOWN

1 Fruit-infused wine (7)

2 Cheese from La Mancha (8)

4 Small plates for sharing (5)

THE END OF AN EMPIRE

Get ready to travel the winding roads that led to the end of the British Empire.

ACROSS

3 The leading advocate of India's independence from British rule (6)

4 Returned to China in 1997 (4, 4)

6 Critical 1956 event that weakened British influence (4, 6)

DOWN

1 Dated term for overseas parts of the British Empire (8)

2 Term for division of a country, often leading to conflict (9)

5 Prime Minister who spoke of the "wind of change" (9)

SPORT

ON YOUR MARKS, GET SET, SOLVE!

It's a race to the finish with these clues
about the world's fastest sprinters.

ACROSS

4 You'll cross this when you fill in all the blanks (6, 4)

5 Nickname for Griffith Joyner, fastest woman of all time (3-2)

6 Linford _ _ _ _ _ _ _ _, British runner who won silver in Seoul (8)

DOWN

1 Jamaican sprinter who is lightning fast (5, 4)

2 Footwear for better grip (6)

3 Starting aids for sprinters (6)

PAINTERS, NOT DECORATORS

Brush up on the art world with this palette of famous painters and their masterpieces.

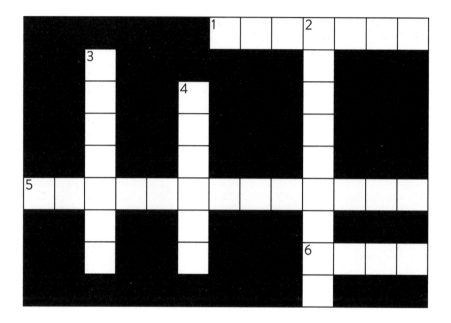

ACROSS

1 Vermeer painted *Girl with a Pearl _ _ _ _ _ _ _* (7)

5 Michelangelo painted this ceiling (7, 6)

6 Surrealist with melting clocks (4)

DOWN

2 Dutch artist known for portraits (9)

3 Spanish master who painted *Guernica* (7)

4 English landscape painter (6)

 **MUSIC**

A COUNTRY MUSIC HOEDOWN

Grab your cowboy boots and tune your banjo;
we're hitting the high notes of country music history!

ACROSS

4 Billy Ray Cyrus had an "Achy _ _ _ _ _ _ _ _ _ _ _" (6, 5)

5 Philanthropist and singer of "Jolene" (5, 6)

6 Canadian country superstar: _ _ _ _ _ _ Twain (6)

DOWN

1 Outlaw country icon: _ _ _ _ _ _ Nelson (6)

2 John Denver asked these to "Take Me Home" (7, 5)

3 This "Man in Black" sang about a "Ring of Fire" (6, 4)

PET LOVERS, ASSEMBLE!

Time for a purrfect puzzle on the world of our furry (and not-so-furry) friends.

ACROSS

1 Man's best friend (3)

4 Known for having nine lives (3)

5 Small Australian bird (6)

6 A wheel-running rodent (7)

DOWN

2 Used to be won at fairs (8)

3 A talkative bird (6)

BEAM ME UP, PUZZLER!

Time to teleport to your spaceship and explore a galaxy of science fiction movies.

ACROSS

1 A dream within a dream (9)

3 Jeff Bridges rides a lightcycle (4)

5 It happened in a galaxy far, far away (4, 4)

6 A cyborg assassin is sent to the past (3, 10)

DOWN

2 Neo's spoon-bending reality (3, 6)

4 Detroit's cyborg lawman (7)

EIGHTIES FASHION

From shoulder pads to scrunchies, the eighties were big, bold and colourful. Here are some highlights.

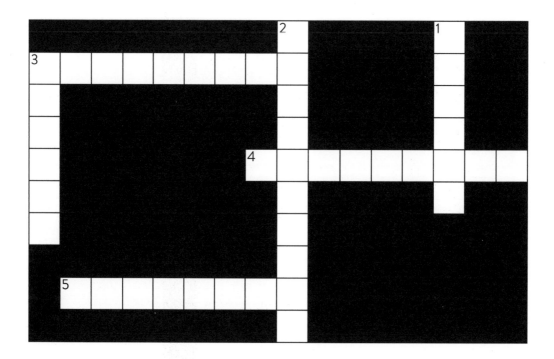

ACROSS

3 Series featuring Don Johnson's rolled-up suit sleeves (5, 4)

4 An American bumbag (5, 4)

5 Famous wearer of parachute pants (2, 6)

DOWN

1 *Top Gun* sunglasses brand (3-3)

2 Dance favourites in *Fame* and *Footloose* (3, 7)

3 Hair that's business in the front, party in the back (6)

EARTH'S GREATEST HITS

How many of these natural wonders
are on your bucket list?

ACROSS

3 Plain English for the aurora borealis (8, 6)

5 Country to the south of the Sahara Desert (5)

6 The Earth's "lungs" in South America (6, 10)

DOWN

1 African plain, scene of a great migration (9)

2 Coral wonderland Down Under (5, 7, 4)

4 Arizona's vertiginous marvel (5, 6)

FOOD AND DRINK

CULINARY BRANDS

Pour yourself a drink and grab a snack. This crossword is all about the brands that have been filling our cupboards and fridges for decades.

ACROSS

2 British chocolatier with a purple touch (7)

3 Soup-maker, with condensed and creamed varieties (9)

5 Dark Irish brew (8)

6 Ketchup kingpin (5)

DOWN

1 Orange juice you might find at a club? (9)

4 A lemon-lime soda fairy (6)

REBELLION THROUGH THE AGES

From fields and trenches to palaces and cities, can you solve the clues for these civil wars that have shaped nations?

ACROSS

4 _ _ _ _ _ _ Rising: Irish event leading to civil war (6)

5 Winners of the Russian Civil War (10)

6 Kenyan anti-colonial rebel group (3, 3)

DOWN

1 Address of a decisive battle in the American Civil War (10)

2 Home to the Tamil Tigers (3, 5)

3 Leader of the Roundheads in the English Civil War (8)

SPORT

A CYCLING TOUR DE FORCE

Strap on your helmet and get ready to cycle through the world of famous cyclists and iconic tours. No training wheels allowed!

ACROSS

1 Main group of cyclists riding together in a race (7)

4 Where the Giro tour takes place (5)

5 Disgraced multiple Tour de France winner (9)

6 Jersey worn by the leader of the Tour de France (6)

DOWN

2 Race against the clock (4, 5)

3 Bradley _ _ _ _ _ _ _: the first British Tour de France winner (7)

BESTSELLING BOOKS

Grab your reading glasses and dive into the literary world of page-turners and bestsellers.

ACROSS

3 Cormac McCarthy's post-apocalyptic tale (3, 4)

5 *To Kill a _ _ _ _ _ _ _ _ _ _ _*: Harper Lee's classic on racial injustice (11)

6 Suzanne Collins' dystopian series (3, 6, 5)

DOWN

1 Author of *Midnight's Children* (6, 7)

2 _ _ _ _ _ _ _ _ _ _ *in the Rye*, J. D. Salinger's tale of teenage angst (3, 7)

4 Author of *The Da Vinci Code* (3, 5)

CROONERS AND DIVAS

Warm up those vocal cords and let's see if you can hit the high notes on this puzzle.

ACROSS

2 "I Will Always Love You" diva (7, 7)

3 French chanteuse of the album *La Vie en Rose* (5, 4)

5 Ol' Blue Eyes himself (5, 7)

6 Johnny _ _ _ _ _ _ had a Christmas No.1 with "When a Child is Born" (6)

DOWN

1 Singer of "What a Wonderful World" (5, 9)

4 Shirley _ _ _ _ _ _, sang theme songs for Bond movies *Goldfinger* and *Diamonds Are Forever* (6)

A BUG'S LIFE

Can you fly through these clues or will you be stuck like a bug on a windscreen?

ACROSS

4 Night-time serenader (7)

6 Famous for its devout posture (7, 6)

DOWN

1 Nature's miniature lantern (7)

2 Picnic crasher (3)

3 Wood's worst enemy (7)

5 Biblical swarmer (6)

MOVIES AND TV

TOON IN, TUNE OUT

Remember when Saturday mornings were all about cereal and cartoons? Relive the magic, one clue at a time.

ACROSS

3 "By the power of Grayskull!" (2-3)

4 Bedrock's modern Stone Age family (3, 11)

5 Mystery-solving Great Dane (6-3)

6 Power-up for pop-eyed sailors (7)

DOWN

1 Blue inhabitant of a magical village (5)

2 Futuristic family with a robot maid (3, 7)

JOYSTICK JUMBLE

Step into a virtual world of fun and challenge your knowledge of computer games.

ACROSS

3 Table tennis in pixel form (4)

5 The original alien shooter (5, 8)

6 Nintendo's famous plumber (5)

DOWN

1 Block-dropping puzzle game (6)

2 Barrel-throwing ape (6, 4)

4 Arcade character who has an appetite for dots (3-3)

SOUTH OF THE BORDER

Get your boots on, it's time to journey through the amazing landscapes of South America.

ACROSS

3 The world's highest uninterrupted waterfall (5, 5)

4 Region shared by Argentina and Chile – and a clothing brand (9)

5 Vast grassy plains in Argentina (6)

6 Inca citadel in the Andes (5, 6)

DOWN

1 The longest mountain range in the world (5)

2 "Music and passion were always the fashion" at this famous Rio beach (10)

FOOD AND DRINK

MORE TEA, VICAR?

Get ready for these tea-time teasers, steeped in picture-postcard British afternoon tea traditions.

ACROSS

2 Monarch known for popularizing afternoon tea (5, 8)

4 Classic and refreshing sandwich filling (8)

5 Essential kit for brewing a proper "cuppa" (6)

6 Toasted and served with butter – it's full of holes! (7)

DOWN

1 Rich and thick topping with berry jam on scones (7, 5)

3 A fragrant black tea with bergamot flavour (4, 4)

ANCIENT ROME

All roads lead to Rome – and this crossword!
Grab your laurel wreath and let the games begin.

ACROSS

4 Fiery neighbour of Pompeii (8)

5 Arena warrior (9)

6 Roman party attire (4)

DOWN

1 Watery Roman engineering marvel (8)

2 Roman army unit (6)

3 Type of races held at the Circus Maximus (7)

AMERICAN FOOTBALL

It's time to huddle up – are you a true gridiron guru?

ACROSS

1 They're in charge on offence (11)

3 The Big Game, usually in February (5, 4)

5 Scoring area at either end of the field (3, 4)

6 Old-school term for the football itself (7)

DOWN

2 Six-point score (9)

4 Famous team from Dallas (7)

SCIENCE FICTION

It's a crossword, Jim, but not as we know it. Set phasers to "solve"!

ACROSS

2 Author of *1984* (6, 6)

3 Frank Herbert's desert-based epic (4)

4 Weir's stranded astronaut story (3, 7)

5 Douglas Adams' Ford Prefect was one (10)

6 L'Engle's mind-bending *A _ _ _ _ _ _ _ in Time* (7)

DOWN

1 Asimov's series with psychohistory (10)

MOTOWN MAGIC

Sharpen your wits, because this Motown-themed crossword will get your brain dancing!

ACROSS

4 Group known for "Reach Out I'll Be There" (4, 4)

5 Stevie, the child prodigy turned legend (6)

6 He asked "What's Going On?" (6, 4)

DOWN

1 Founder of the Motown label (5, 5)

2 _ _ _ _ _ _ Robinson, of Miracles fame (6)

3 Diana Ross's original group (8)

BIRDS OF A FEATHER

Spread your mental wings and prepare for take-off as we soar through the skies of the animal kingdom.

ACROSS

5 Insect known for its hovering ability (9)

6 "One for sorrow, two for joy" (6)

DOWN

1 Urban aviator with a homing instinct (6)

2 Large scavenger of the Andes (6)

3 Bird with a built-in fishing net (7)

4 This mammal really flies (3)

CLASSIC UK SITCOMS

Goodness gracious me, it's puzzle time!

ACROSS

2 Cunning character played by Rowan Atkinson (10)

3 A pint of blood is very nearly this, according to Tony Hancock (2, 6)

5 *Keeping Up Appearances* matriarch (8)

6 Spike Milligan's radio comedy (3, 4, 4)

DOWN

1 Basil's chaotic hotel (6, 6)

4 Cockney entrepreneur in Peckham (3, 3)

POPULAR CULTURE

CELEBRITY COUPLES

Time for a double date through Hollywood and beyond!

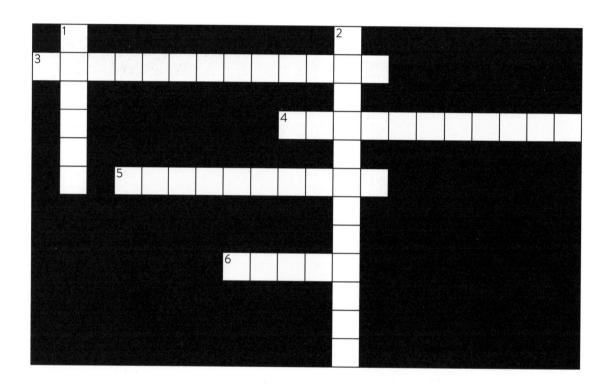

ACROSS

3 Married twice to Elizabeth Taylor (7, 6)

4 Music and peace protests united them in the sixties (4, 3, 4)

5 Portmanteau name for Pitt and Jolie (10)

6 Bonnie's infamous partner (5)

DOWN

1 Aussie who loved a Cruise? (6)

2 David and Victoria, in other words (4, 3, 5)

 **GEOGRAPHY**

WHEN NATURE GETS MAD

Can you tackle the might and fury of Mother Earth?

ACROSS

1 Country of fiery Eyjafjallajökull eruption, which caused air-traffic chaos in 2010 (7)

5 Plague that wiped out a third of Europe (5, 5)

6 Oceanic wave that leaves others in the shade (7)

DOWN

2 American ecological disaster in the thirties (4, 4)

3 Volcanic eruption heard around the world in 1883 (8)

4 Buried by Vesuvius (7)

FOOD AND DRINK

SPICE UP YOUR LIFE

Whet your appetite with this puzzle about delicious Indian cuisine.

ACROSS

3 Oven for certain marinated meats (7)

5 Smoothie-like mango drink (5)

6 Fried vegetable snack (5)

DOWN

1 Indian bread (7)

2 Flavourful rice dish, often with chicken or lamb (7)

4 South Indian pancake (4)

THE VIETNAM WAR

The conflict lasted nearly 20 years but what can you remember about this struggle between north and south?

ACROSS

1 US president during the war's later years (5)

3 Nickname of the Bell UH-1 Iroquois helicopter (4)

4 North Vietnam leader 1945–69 (2, 3, 4)

DOWN

1 Jellied gasoline used as a weapon (6)

2 Old name of the South Vietnam capital (6)

3 Capital city since reunification in 1976 (5)

WORLD OF SPORT

Break a mental sweat with this tour of some of the world's most unusual "sports".

ACROSS

3 Indian game of tag and breath-holding (7)

5 Smelly race at Cooper's Hill in Gloucestershire (6-7)

6 Horse-chestnut combat (7)

DOWN

1 Irish field sport resembling hockey (7)

2 Sport from the wizarding world (9)

4 To Zorb is to roll downhill or exercise in a giant _ _ _ _ (4)

IT'S ALL GREEK TO ME

Unearth the gods and heroes of Greek mythology –
but don't get lost in the labyrinth!

ACROSS

2 Jason's crew (9)

5 Opened a box of troubles (7)

6 One-eyed giant (7)

DOWN

1 Half-man, half-bull (8)

3 Number of labours undertaken by Hercules (6)

4 Flew too close to the sun (6)

THE BRITISH ARE COMING!

How well do you remember British music in the US in the sixties?

ACROSS

3 _ _ _ _ _ Springfield of "Son of a Preacher Man" (5)

4 Rolling Stones' frontman (4, 6)

5 Liverpudlian musical movement (10)

6 Fab Four who conquered America (3, 7)

DOWN

1 Eric Clapton's early band (3, 9)

2 Who were the "_ _ _ _ _ _ _ Wizards"! (7)

WHEELS, WINGS AND WATERWAYS

No need for road rage – just enjoy the ride through the world of transportation.

ACROSS

4 Fictional skateboard from 1985's *Back to the Future* (10)

5 Unmanned aerial vehicle (5)

6 Single-track railway (8)

DOWN

1 Train without wheels (6)

2 Faster than sound (10)

3 Vehicle powered by liquid fuel and electricity (6)

LIGHTS, CAMERA, CROSSWORD!

It's time for your close-up – let's test
your knowledge on movie stars!

ACROSS

2 She was "Somewhere Over
the Rainbow" (4, 7)

3 This devil wore Prada (5, 6)

5 *Pillow Talk's* romantic
lead (5, 3)

6 He'll always have Paris (8, 6)

DOWN

1 Put in a *Titanic* performance
as Rose (4, 7)

4 Sidney _ _ _ _ _ _ _, star
of *Guess Who's Coming
to Dinner?* (7)

POPULAR CULTURE

BRAND-NAME TEASERS

Can you match up these well-known tag lines with their equally famous brands?

ACROSS

5 The number of cats who prefer Whiskas (5, 3, 2, 3)

6 "Think different" (5)

DOWN

1 "I'm lovin' it" (9)

2 "Just do it" (4)

3 "Because you're worth it" (6)

4 "Beanz Meanz _ _ _ _ _" (5)

GEOGRAPHY

RIVER DANCE

Grab your paddle, it's time to take a trip down the world's most famous rivers.

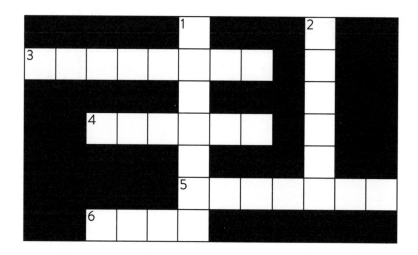

ACROSS

3 River that carved the Grand Canyon (8)

4 Holy river of India (6)

5 Source of the Victoria Falls in Africa (7)

6 Agatha Christie plotted a death on this river (4)

DOWN

1 China's longest river (7)

2 Strauss wrote that it was blue (6)

FOOD AND DRINK

CHRISTMAS FEASTS

Tease your taste buds with this culinary
sleigh ride around Europe.

ACROSS

4 Dutch custard-
coloured liqueur (8)

6 Sweet British fare, no
meat involved! (5, 3)

DOWN

1 Christmas hot drink made
with red wine and spices (6, 4)

2 Preferred fowl for
Germany's feast (5)

3 Sparkling wine drunk
in Spain (4)

5 Iconic Christmas fish in
Eastern Europe (4)

STARS AND STRIPES

From Washington's wig to modern politics, get ready to untangle the threads of America's past.

ACROSS

2 US president assassinated in Dallas (7)

4 Document ratified in 1787 setting the framework for the US (12)

5 Famous protest against British taxes (6, 3, 5)

6 Era when the sale of alcohol was illegal (11)

DOWN

1 Home state of President Clinton (8)

3 Proclamation that declared the freedom of slaves (12)

SPORT

GOOOOOAAAAAAAAL!

Think you know your football? Time to dive into a world of World Cups.

ACROSS

5 Famous Argentine known for the "Hand of God" (5, 8)

6 First winners of the World Cup (7)

DOWN

1 Award for the tournament's top scorer (6, 4)

2 Jules _ _ _ _ _ _ _ _: original World Cup trophy (5, 3)

3 Only country to play in every final (6)

4 Brazilian football legend with three World Cup titles (4)

TITANS OF LITERATURE

If you've ever found solace in the quiet pages of a book, this puzzle is for you.

ACROSS

3 Creator of Tom Sawyer and Huckleberry Finn (4, 5)

5 Darcy's creator (4, 6)

6 Frenchman with a "hunchback" hero (6, 4)

DOWN

1 His hero turned into a bug (5, 5)

2 Author of *The Bell Jar* (6, 5)

4 She wrote *Middlemarch*, last name Eliot, as a pseudonym (6)

SOUNDS OF THE SEVENTIES

Step into the groove as you head back to an era of bell-bottoms and classic anthems.

ACROSS

3 Historical Eurovision hit for ABBA (8)

4 The Eagles could never leave here (5, 10)

5 Don _ _ _ _ _ _ sang about "the day the music died" (6)

6 Queen's operatic "Rhapsody" (8)

DOWN

1 Led Zeppelin's route "to heaven" (8)

2 Elton John's cosmic voyager (6, 3)

ANSWERS

p.4:
3. *THE BRADY BUNCH* 5. *MASH*
6. *SEINFELD* 1. LUCILLE BALL
2. CHEERS 4. FONZIE

p.5:
4. ATM 6. POCKET CALCULATOR
1. MINI SKIRT 2. PACEMAKER
3. EIGHT 5. KEVLAR

p.6:
3. CANBERRA 5. INDIA
6. WASHINGTON, DC 1. BUENOS
AIRES 2. BONN 4. CAIRO

p.7:
1. BORSCHT 4. SUSHI 5. BAKLAVA
6. BRATWURST 2. CROISSANT
3.PAELLA

p.8:
1. MISSILE CRISIS 4. MCCARTHYISM
5. BERLIN WALL 6. GLASNOST
2. IRON CURTAIN 3. ARMS RACE

p.9:
3. CASSIUS CLAY 4. LONG JUMP
6. PHELPS 1. FOSBURY FLOP
2. MARY DECKER 5. NADIA

p.10:
3. TOAD HALL 5. ASLAN
6. WONDERLAND 1. GREEN GABLES
2. MOWGLI 4. LOST BOYS

p.11:
3. INFERNO 4. *YMCA* 5. BEE GEES
6. GLORIA GAYNOR 1. DONNA
SUMMER 2. *NIGHT FEVER*

p.12:
1. GAGARIN 6. CHALLENGER
2. ARMSTRONG 3. HUBBLE
4. SPUTNIK 5. VOYAGER

p.13:
2. *PLAYBOY* 4. BASEBALL 5. *SOME
LIKE IT HOT* 6. KENNEDY 1. NORMA
JEANE 3. WARHOL

p.14:
4. *CATS* 5. *OKLAHOMA* 6. *SWEENEY
TODD* 1. *MY FAIR LADY* 2. ABBA
3. *WICKED*

p.15:
5. COLOSSEUM 6. STATUE OF
LIBERTY 1. GREAT WALL 2. TAJ
MAHAL 3. STONEHENGE 4. EIFFEL

p.16:
4. PIÑA COLADA 5. MANHATTAN
6. OLD FASHIONED
1. COSMOPOLITAN 2. MARGARITA
3. MARTINI

p.17:
3. GANDHI 5. CHAIRMAN
6. ROOSEVELT 1. LENIN 2. MANDELA
4. DE GAULLE

p.18:
4. MCENROE 5. WIMBLEDON
6. CLAY 1. BACKHAND 2. FEDERER
3. SERENA

p.19:
1. ORWELL 2. GREAT BRITAIN
4. THEROUX 5. *INNOCENTS*
1. *ON THE ROAD* 3. EIGHTY

p.20:
4. *THE NUTCRACKER* 5. WAGNER
6. *CARMEN* 1. MOZART
2. BEETHOVEN 3. *SEASONS*

p.21:
3. FLOPPY 5. ASK JEEVES 6. ATARI
1. MICROSOFT 2. MYSPACE
4. SPECTRUM

p.42:
2. YELLOWSTONE 4. REDWOOD TREE 5. GRAND 6. YOSEMITE 1. DEATH VALLEY 3. EVERGLADES

p.43:
3. MADELEINE 5. COQ AU VIN 6. TARTE TATIN 1. MARSEILLE 2. CASSOULET 4. ALMOND

p.44:
3. NAGASAKI 4. ENIGMA 5. EISENHOWER 6. DUNKIRK 1. STALINGRAD 2. VICHY

p.45:
2. PELÉ 3. ITALY 5. GEORGE BEST 6. BECKENBAUER 1. KEEGAN 4. TOTAL

p.46:
6. ORIENT EXPRESS 1. HAMMETT 2. POIROT 3. SAYERS 4. MARPLE 5. WATSON

p.47:
3. LED ZEPPELIN 5. ROLLING STONES 6. DAVID BOWIE 1. *THE WALL* 2. BLACK SABBATH 4. MERCURY

p.48:
1. PENICILLIN 4. PLACEBO 5. CLONE 1. PACEMAKER 2. INSULIN 3. IVF

p.49:
2. ELM STREET 4. HALLOWEEN 5. *THE OMEN* 6. FRANKENSTEIN 1. *PSYCHO* 3. *THE SHINING*

p.50:
3. PEPSI 4. KFC 5. ALKA-SELTZER 6. GILLETTE 1. MAYBELLINE 2. COCA-COLA

p.51:
2. RED SEA 5. GULF STREAM 6. DEAD SEA 1. SARGASSO 3. BLACK SEA 4. PACIFIC

p.52:
4. MARS 5. TOBLERONE 6. MARATHON 1. GOBSTOPPER 2. JELLY 3. HARIBO

p.53:
3. WATERGATE 5. *NEWS OF THE WORLD* 6. CASH FOR 1. IRAN-CONTRA 2. LEWINSKY 4. PROFUMO

p.54:
3. AUGUSTA 4. GREG NORMAN 5. RYDER CUP 6. SEVE BALLESTEROS 1. JACK NICKLAUS 2. ST ANDREWS

p.55:
3. BRIDGET JONES 5. *GONE WITH THE WIND* 6. SHAWSHANK 1. *JURASSIC PARK* 2. *THE GODFATHER* 4. *FIGHT CLUB*

p.56:
3. BILLIE 5. *GREAT BALLS OF FIRE* 6. ROCKABILLY 1. ELVIS PRESLEY 2. FITZGERALD 4. MOTOWN

p.57:
4. KOALA 5. PALM 6. BONSAI 1. WILLOW 2. BAOBAB 3. MAPLE

p.58:
2. *FANTASIA* 4. THUMPER 5. SNOW WHITE 6. ROBIN HOOD 1. DALMATIAN 3. ALADDIN

p.59:
1. HASHTAG 4. FOLLOWER 6. TRENDING 2. ALGORITHM 3. RETWEET 5. LIKE

p.60:
4. ANTARCTICA 5. UTAH 6. OASIS 1. KALAHARI 2. SAHARA 3. CAMEL

p.61:
1. PANETTONE 3. ESPRESSO 5. CALZONE 6. RISOTTO 2. OSSO BUCO 4. PESTO

p.62:
3. COMMUNES 4. *LITTLE RED BOOK* 5. PURGE 6. RED GUARD 1. PERSONALITY 2. PEKING

p.63:
5. *LEAGUE* 6. WORLD SERIES 1. BABE 2. *MONEYBALL* 3. YANKEES 4. PITCHER

p.64:
1. SMITHSONIAN 4. LOUVRE 6. BRITISH MUSEUM 2. METROPOLITAN 3. GUGGENHEIM 5. TATE

p.65:
3. BRITANNIA 4. JARVIS COCKER 5. GALLAGHER 6. VERVE 1. *PARKLIFE* 2. BRIT AWARDS

p.66:
1. BARNACLE 3. SEAHORSE 4. NARWHAL 5. CORAL REEF 1. BLUE WHALE 5. KRILL

p.67:
3. *THE GREAT ESCAPE* 4. VIETNAM 5. *THE DIRTY DOZEN* 6. U-BOAT 1. *APOCALYPSE NOW* 2. PRIVATE RYAN

p.68:
2. WII 4. MICROSOFT 6. BLU-RAY 1. BLACKBERRY 3. IPOD 5. PILOT

p.69:
5. SANTORINI 6. PARIS 1. HAWAII 2. BALI 3. TAHITI 4. KYOTO

p.70:
1. CRÊPE SUZETTE 4. PAVLOVA 5. DOUGHNUT 1. CHURRO 2. TIRAMISU 3. STOLLEN

p.71:
2. NORMAN 3. OIL 5. DESERT STORM 1. NO FLY ZONE 4. SADDAM 6. SCUD

p.72:
4. EDWARDS 5. LIONS 6. HAKA 1. FULL-BACK 2. RED CARD 3. TRIES

p.73:
3. *SHŌGUN* 4. *WOLF HALL* 6. *THE NAME OF THE ROSE* 1. *MUSKETEERS* 2. *WAR AND PEACE* 5. BUTLER

p.74:
2. *THE MOON* 4. FLEETWOOD MAC 5. PAUL SIMON 6. *BORN TO RUN* 1. *WHAT'S GOING ON* 3. *ABBEY ROAD*

p.75:
3. MILKY WAY 5. SOLAR FLARE 6. RED 1. BLACK HOLE 2. JUPITER 4. ASTEROID

p.76:
2. MEL BROOKS 4. ROBIN WILLIAMS 5. BOB HOPE 6. WHOOPI GOLDBERG 1. GOLDIE HAWN 3. TINA FEY

p.77:
3. *FUNNY GIRL* 5. ANDY WARHOL 6. ELIZABETH TAYLOR 1. BALLET DANCER 2. JIMI HENDRIX 4. BOB DYLAN

p.78:
4. BEIJING 5. ARABIAN SEA 6. SAMURAI 1. MONGOLIA 2. SILK ROAD 3. SIBERIA

p.79:
3. GAZPACHO 5. FABADA 6. CHORIZO 1. SANGRIA 2. MANCHEGO 4. TAPAS

p.80:
3. GANDHI 4. HONG KONG 6. SUEZ CRISIS 1. COLONIES 2. PARTITION 5. MACMILLAN

p.81:
4. FINISH LINE 5. FLO-JO
6. CHRISTIE 1. USAIN BOLT 2. SPIKES
3. BLOCKS

p.82:
1. *EARRING* 5. SISTINE CHAPEL
6. DALI 2. REMBRANDT 3. PICASSO
4. TURNER

p.83:
4. *BREAKY HEART* 5. DOLLY PARTON
6. SHANIA 1. WILLIE
2. *COUNTRY ROADS*
3. JOHNNY CASH

p.84:
1. DOG 4. CAT 5. BUDGIE
6. HAMSTER 2. GOLDFISH
3. PARROT

p.85:
1. *INCEPTION* 3. *TRON* 5. *STAR WARS*
6. *THE TERMINATOR* 2. *THE MATRIX*
4. *ROBOCOP*

p.86:
3. *MIAMI VICE* 4. FANNY PACK
5. MC HAMMER 1. RAY-BAN 2. LEG
WARMERS 3. MULLET

p.87:
3. NORTHERN LIGHTS 5. SUDAN
6. AMAZON RAINFOREST
1. SERENGETI 2. GREAT BARRIER
REEF 4. GRAND CANYON

p.88:
2. CADBURY 3. CAMPBELL'S
5. GUINNESS 6. HEINZ
1. TROPICANA 4. SPRITE

p.89:
4. EASTER 5. BOLSHEVIKS 6. MAU
MAU 1. GETTYSBURG 2. SRI LANKA
3. CROMWELL

p.90:
1. PELOTON 4. ITALY 5. ARMSTRONG
6. YELLOW 2. TIME TRIAL 3. WIGGINS

p.91:
3. *THE ROAD* 5. *MOCKINGBIRD*
6. *THE HUNGER GAMES* 1. SALMAN
RUSHDIE 2. *THE CATCHER* 4. DAN
BROWN

p.92:
2. WHITNEY HOUSTON 3. EDITH
PIAF 5. FRANK SINATRA 6. MATHIS
1. LOUIS ARMSTRONG 4. BASSEY

p.93:
4. CRICKET 6. PRAYING MANTIS
1. FIREFLY 2. ANT 3. TERMITE
5. LOCUST

p.94:
3. HE-MAN 4. *THE FLINTSTONES*
5. SCOOBY DOO 6. SPINACH
1. SMURF 2. *THE JETSONS*

p.95:
3. *PONG* 5. *SPACE INVADERS*
6. MARIO 1. *TETRIS* 2. DONKEY KONG
4. PAC-MAN

p.96:
3. ANGEL FALLS 4. PATAGONIA
5. PAMPAS 6. MACHU PICCHU
1. ANDES 2. COPACABANA

p.97:
2. QUEEN VICTORIA 4. CUCUMBER
5. TEAPOT 6. CRUMPET 1. CLOTTED
CREAM 3. EARL GREY

p.98:
4. VESUVIUS 5. GLADIATOR
6. TOGA 1. AQUEDUCT 2. LEGION
3. CHARIOT

p.99:
1. QUARTERBACK 3. SUPER BOWL
5. END ZONE 6. PIGSKIN
2. TOUCHDOWN 4. COWBOYS

p.100:
2. GEORGE ORWELL 3. *DUNE* 4. *THE
MARTIAN* 5. HITCHHIKER 6. *WRINKLE*
1. *FOUNDATION*

p.101:
4. FOUR TOPS 5. WONDER
6. MARVIN GAYE 1. BERRY GORDY
2. SMOKEY 3. SUPREMES

p.102:
5. DRAGONFLY 6. MAGPIE
1. PIGEON 2. CONDOR 3. PELICAN
4. BAT

p.103:
2. BLACKADDER 3. AN ARMFUL
5. HYACINTH 6. *THE GOON SHOW*
1. FAWLTY TOWERS 4. DEL BOY

p.104:
3. RICHARD BURTON 4. JOHN AND
YOKO 5. BRANGELINA 6. CLYDE
1. KIDMAN 2. POSH AND BECKS

p.105:
1. ICELAND 5. BLACK DEATH
6. TSUNAMI 2. DUST BOWL
3. KRAKATOA 4. POMPEII

p.106:
3. TANDOOR 5. LASSI 6. BHAJI
1. CHAPATI 2. BIRYANI 4. DOSA

p.107:
1. NIXON 3. HUEY 4. HO CHI MINH
1. NAPALM 2. SAIGON 3. HANOI

p.108:
3. KABADDI 5. CHEESE-ROLLING
6. CONKERS 1. HURLING
2. QUIDDITCH 4. BALL

p.109:
2. ARGONAUTS 5. PANDORA
6. CYCLOPS 1. MINOTAUR 3. TWELVE
4. ICARUS

p.110:
3. DUSTY 4. MICK JAGGER
5. MERSEYBEAT 6. THE BEATLES
1. THE YARDBIRDS 2. PINBALL

p.111:
4. HOVERBOARD 5. DRONE
6. MONORAIL 1. MAGLEV
2. SUPERSONIC 3. HYBRID

p.112:
2. JUDY GARLAND 3. MERYL STREEP
5. DORIS DAY 6. HUMPHREY
BOGART 1. KATE WINSLET
4. POITIER

p.113:
5. EIGHT OUT OF TEN 6. APPLE
1. MCDONALD'S 2. NIKE 3. L'ORÉAL
4. HEINZ

p.114:
3. COLORADO 4. GANGES
5. ZAMBEZI 6. NILE 1. YANGTZE
2. DANUBE

p.115:
4. ADVOCAAT 6. MINCE PIE
1. MULLED WINE 2. GOOSE 3. CAVA
5. CARP

p.116:
2. KENNEDY 4. CONSTITUTION
5. BOSTON TEA PARTY
6. PROHIBITION 1. ARKANSAS
3. EMANCIPATION

p.117:
5. DIEGO MARADONA 6. URUGUAY
1. GOLDEN BOOT 2. RIMET CUP
3. BRAZIL 4. PELÉ

p.118:
3. MARK TWAIN 5. JANE AUSTEN
6. VICTOR HUGO 1. FRANZ KAFKA
2. SYLVIA PLATH 4. GEORGE

p.119:
3. *WATERLOO* 4. *HOTEL CALIFORNIA*
5. MCLEAN 6. BOHEMIAN
1. STAIRWAY 2. *ROCKET MAN*

The Retirement Puzzle Book

Activities and Games to Keep Your Mind Active

Paperback

978-1-80007-839-0

This collection of verbal and visual challenges will help you stay sharp and stimulated as you embark on a new chapter in life

Retirement is incredibly rich with possibilities – it's just a question of how to fill all that free time. Well, now that you've earned many an hour of peaceful freedom, how about a puzzle or two to prove you're still as clever as you always were?

From quick-fire trivia questions to more leisurely crosswords and sudoku, whether you're a recent retiree, approaching the big day or have been enjoying your freedom for years, there's plenty in these pages to keep you busy and set your mind purring.

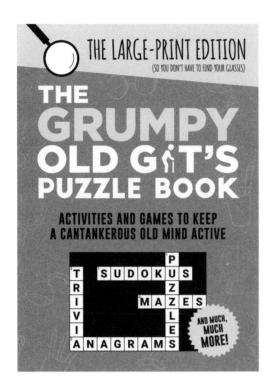

The Grumpy Old Git's Puzzle Book

Activities and Games to Keep a Catankerous Old Mind Active

Paperback

978-1-80007-105-6

Warning: this puzzle book may cause enjoyment and momentary loss of grumpiness

The world has gone to hell in a handbasket and everyone around you is a fool. What you need is something to take your mind off it all.

Grumble your way through these word searches, sudokus, crosswords, spot the differences, quizzes and mazes and you'll find your crabbiness melting away – until you get stumped by a silly anagram, that is!

Have you enjoyed this book? If so, find us on Facebook at **Summersdale Publishers**, on Twitter/X at **@Summersdale** and on Instagram and TikTok at **@summersdalebooks** and get in touch. We'd love to hear from you!

www.summersdale.com

IMAGE CREDITS